NOTHIN

LIKE AI

MAILBOX

NOTHING ECHOES LIKE AN EMPTY MAILBOX

by Charles M. Schulz

An Owl Book
Henry Holt and Company/ New York

Henry Holt and Company, Inc.
Publishers since 1866
115 West 18th Street
New York, New York 10011

Henry Holt® is a registered trademark
of Henry Holt and Company, Inc.

Published in Canada by Fitzhenry & Whiteside Ltd.,
195 Allstate Parkway, Markham, Ontario L3R 4T8.

Library of Congress Catalog Card Number: 95-79326

ISBN 0-8050-3936-8 (An Owl Book: pbk.)

Henry Holt books are available for special promotions
and premiums. For details contact: Director, Special Markets.

Originally published by Holt, Rinehart and Winston in two
expanded editions under the titles *And a Woodstock in a
Birch Tree* in 1978 and *Here Comes the April Fool!* in 1980.

New Owl Book Edition—1995

Printed in the United States of America
All first editions are printed on acid-free paper.∞

1 3 5 7 9 10 8 6 4 2

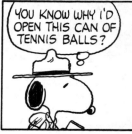

TODAY IS GEORGE WASHINGTON'S BIRTHDAY

IF HE WERE ALIVE TODAY, THEY'D PROBABLY BE HAVING A BIG PARTY FOR HIM AT MOUNT VERNON

THAT, HOWEVER, NEED NOT CONCERN ANYONE IN THIS CLASSROOM

YOU WOULDN'T HAVE BEEN INVITED ANYWAY!

SCHULZ

I HATE BEING A NOTHING! I REFUSE TO GO THROUGH THE REST OF MY LIFE AS A ZERO!

WHAT WOULD YOU LIKE TO BE, CHARLIE BROWN, A FIVE? OR HOW ABOUT A TWENTY-SIX? OR A PAR SEVENTY-TWO?

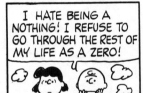

I KNOW WHAT YOU COULD BE, CHARLIE BROWN.. A SQUARE ROOT!

I THINK YOU'D MAKE A GREAT SQUARE ROOT, CHARLIE BROWN..

I CAN'T STAND IT!

SCHULZ

YES, MA'AM, I'M AWAKE! THE MOVIE? OH, YES, MA'AM, THE MOVIE WAS GREAT!

WHAT WAS IT ABOUT? WELL, UH... IT WAS... WELL, I THINK....

I DON'T SUPPOSE IT WAS ABOUT DONNY AND MARIE, WAS IT?

I'VE BEEN THINKING ABOUT YOUR PROBLEM, SIR

MAYBE YOU FALL ASLEEP IN CLASS BECAUSE OF UNCORRECTED ASTIGMATISM...

OH, SURE! YOU'D LOVE TO SEE ME WEARING GLASSES, WOULDN'T YOU, MARCIE?

SOME OF US THINK WE LOOK KIND OF CUTE WITH OUR GLASSES, SIR!

HEY, CHUCK, THIS IS GONNA CRACK YOU UP! ARE YOU LISTENING?

MARCIE HAS THIS THEORY ABOUT WHY I FALL ASLEEP IN SCHOOL ALL THE TIME...IT'S A WILD THEORY..WAIT'LL YOU HEAR IT...IT'S REALLY WILD...

HEE HEE HEE

WELL, MARCIE'S USUALLY RIGHT ABOUT A LOT OF THINGS..SHE'S PRETTY SHARP

DO YOU LOVE ME, CHUCK?

SCHULZ

I CALLED HIM LAST NIGHT, MARCIE... I CALLED CHUCK, AND I ASKED HIM IF HE LOVES ME...

THAT STUPID CHUCK!! HE DIDN'T EVEN KNOW WHAT TO SAY!

I THOUGHT TALKING TO HIM ON THE PHONE WOULD HELP...

SOMETIMES, IF YOU TALK TO SOMEONE ON THE PHONE LONG ENOUGH, THEY'LL FORGET YOU HAVE A BIG NOSE!

SCHULZ

ONE MOMENT, PLEASE...

WE INTERRUPT OUR REGULAR PROGRAM TO BRING YOU THIS SPECIAL BULLETIN

IT'S A NICE DAY OUTSIDE

I'VE ALWAYS BEEN CRITICIZED

RIGHT FROM THE BEGINNING!

RIGHT FROM THE VERY FIRST DAY I WAS BORN...

THEY SAID I WASN'T RIGHT FOR THE PART!

 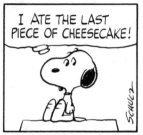

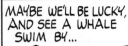

FORGET IT!

IF THERE'S ANYTHING MY DOGHOUSE DOESN'T NEED, IT'S A HOOD ORNAMENT

TRUE...FALSE...

TRUE...TRUE... FALSE...TRUE...

MA'AM?

WHAT DO WE DO IF WE COME ACROSS A HALF-TRUTH?

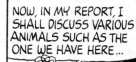

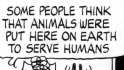

No.1
CRAB

SLAM!

BOY, DO I FEEL CRABBY!

MAYBE I CAN BE OF HELP

WHY DON'T YOU JUST TAKE MY PLACE HERE IN FRONT OF THE TV WHILE I GO AND FIX YOU A NICE SNACK?

SOMETIMES WE ALL NEED A LITTLE PAMPERING TO HELP US FEEL BETTER...

SEE? I CAME RIGHT BACK! HERE'S A NICE SANDWICH FOR YOU, SOME CHOCOLATE CHIP COOKIES AND A COLD GLASS OF MILK...

NOW, IS THERE ANYTHING ELSE I CAN GET YOU?

IS THERE ANYTHING I HAVEN'T THOUGHT OF?

YES, THERE'S ONE THING THAT YOU HAVEN'T THOUGHT OF.....

I DON'T WANNA FEEL BETTER!!

C C C C C C

THESE ARE C'S! THEY'RE VERY IMPORTANT IF YOU OWN A CAT...

IF YOU OWN A CAT?

WHEN YOU WRITE TO A FRIEND ABOUT YOUR CAT, YOU HAVE TO KNOW HOW TO MAKE GOOD C'S

THEY HAVE OTHER USES, TOO, WHICH I CAN EXPLAIN LATER...

I'LL BE AROUND

DO YOU THINK YOU'LL LOVE ME WHEN I'M OLD AND GRAY?

I DON'T KNOW

IF I DON'T LOVE YOU NOW, HOW CAN I LOVE YOU WHEN YOU'RE OLD AND GRAY?

WE'LL SEE!!

OKAY, WE'LL SIT HERE AND WAIT, AND IF YOUR MOTHER FLIES BY, YOU CAN GIVE HER THE FLOWER...

I JUST WISH YOU'D BE MORE REALISTIC

I DON'T THINK YOU'D RECOGNIZE YOUR MOTHER IF YOU SAW HER

YOU THINK SHE'S GOING TO HAVE GRAY HAIR AND BE CARRYING AN APPLE PIE?

SHE COULD PROBABLY FLY RIGHT BY YOUR NOSE, AND YOU'D NEVER RECOGNIZE HER

MOM!!

?

OH, EXCUSE ME! I THOUGHT YOU WERE MY MOM! I BEG YOUR PARDON!

HEE
HEE
HEE
HEE
HEE

WELL, FROM A DISTANCE A ST. BERNARD LOOKS SOMETHING LIKE A BEAGLE

LUCY, DEAR SISTER!

I ALMOST BOUGHT YOU A BIRTHDAY PRESENT JUST NOW

I SAW THIS BOTTLE OF COLOGNE IN A STORE WINDOW, AND IT ONLY COST A DOLLAR...

I KNEW IT WOULD MAKE YOU HAPPY TO GET IT, BUT THEN I SAW SOMETHING THAT I KNEW WOULD MAKE YOU EVEN MORE HAPPY!

IN THE WINDOW OF THE STORE NEXT DOOR, THERE WAS A SALAMI SANDWICH WHICH ALSO COST A DOLLAR...NOW, I KNOW HOW CONCERNED YOU ARE FOR THE PEOPLES OF THIS WORLD...

I KNOW HOW HAPPY IT'S GOING TO MAKE YOU WHEN I BECOME A FAMOUS DOCTOR, AND CAN HELP THE PEOPLE OF THE WORLD

BUT IF I'M GOING TO BECOME A DOCTOR, I'M GOING TO HAVE TO GET GOOD GRADES IN SCHOOL...

AND TO GET GOOD GRADES, I'M GOING TO HAVE TO STUDY, AND IN ORDER TO STUDY, I HAVE TO BE HEALTHY...

IN ORDER TO BE HEALTHY, I HAVE TO EAT...SO INSTEAD OF THE COLOGNE, I BOUGHT THE SANDWICH...ALL FOR YOUR HAPPINESS!

I'M SO HAPPY I COULD CRY!

EEK! EEK! EEK!

I'M PRACTICING MY 'EEKS'

'EEKS'?

'EEKS' ARE VERY IMPORTANT IF YOU'RE WRITING A STORY ABOUT A PRINCESS...

SAY THERE'S THIS BEAUTIFUL PRINCESS. WHO LIVES IN A CASTLE...SHE'S SITTING AT HER LOOM ONE DAY WHEN SUDDENLY A MOUSE RUNS ACROSS THE FLOOR...

"EEK!"
SHE CRIES...

IF YOU'RE DOING A STORY ABOUT A PRINCESS, YOU HAVE TO BE ABLE TO WRITE A GOOD 'EEK'

AN 'AWK' PROBABLY WOULD HAVE KILLED ME!

YOUR SERVE AGAIN, PARTNER

THIS COULD BE GAME POINT

IT ALSO COULD BE SET POINT AND MATCH POINT...

HOW ABOUT CHOKE POINT?

"I HOPE YOU WON'T TAKE UMBRAGE AT WHAT I TELL YOU," SHE SAID

"I NEVER TAKE UMBRAGE," HE REPLIED

"UNLESS, OF COURSE, IT'S LYING AROUND, AND NO ONE ELSE WANTS IT!" HA! HA! HA! HA!

OKAY, ON WITH THE STORY...

THERE'S A STRANGE FEELING OF LONELINESS AFTER A BALL GAME IS OVER...

THE FIELD IS EMPTY... THE AIR IS SILENT... THE SHADOWS BEGIN TO LENGTHEN...

SOON NOTHING IS LEFT BUT MEMORIES

STUPID KID... I DIDN'T THINK HE WAS EVER GOING TO LEAVE!

HOW DID I EVER END UP AS A PITCHER'S MOUND FOR A STUPID KIDS' TEAM?

"GO INTO SPORTS," MY FATHER SAID.."THAT'S WHERE THE MONEY IS!"

WHY COULDN'T I HAVE BEEN A GOLF GREEN AT PEBBLE BEACH OR A GRASS COURT AT WIMBLEDON? STILL, I GUESS IT COULD HAVE BEEN WORSE...

I COULD HAVE BEEN THE PLEXIGLAS BEHIND A HOCKEY NET!

OKAY, MEN! RISE AND SHINE!

LET'S CHOW DOWN, AND GET READY TO HIT THE TRAIL

I KNOW EVERYONE IS TIRED, BUT WE HAVE A LOT OF GROUND TO COVER TODAY...

WHERE'S OLIVIER? HE'S FALLEN BEHIND AGAIN...

WE'LL TRAVEL A WHOLE LOT FASTER, OLIVIER, IF YOU'LL GET OUT OF YOUR SLEEPING BAG!

I SUPPOSE WE SHOULD BE OBSERVING WILDLIFE WHILE WE'RE OUT HERE, SHOULDN'T WE, SIR?

ABSOLUTELY, MARCIE.. THAT'S ONE OF THE PURPOSES OF BACKPACKING

?

LOOK, SIR, I THINK I'VE FOUND A STRANGE CREATURE...IT LOOKS LIKE A GIANT WORM OR SOMETHING...

THAT'S A BIRD IN A SLEEPING BAG, MARCIE! YOU'VE FOUND A BIRD IN A SLEEPING BAG!

I THINK WE'VE DISTURBED THE WILDLIFE, SIR, OR UPSET THE BALANCE OF NATURE OR SOMETHING...

A BIRD IN A SLEEPING BAG?!

WELL, HOW DID THE TRIAL TURN OUT?

THE PROSECUTING ATTORNEY CLAIMED THAT BIRDS OF A FEATHER WILL GATHER TOGETHER?

BUT THE DEFENSE ATTORNEY SAID THAT A BIRD IN THE HAND IS WORTH TWO IN THE BUSH...

YOU'RE RIGHT...A VERY DIFFICULT CASE

I'VE BECOME INTERESTED IN LEARNING ABOUT THE EARTH'S SURFACE

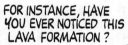

FOR INSTANCE, HAVE YOU EVER NOTICED THIS LAVA FORMATION?

ANCIENT LAVA FLOWS SUCH AS THIS ONE HERE ARE REALLY QUITE FASCINATING

I ALWAYS THOUGHT THIS WAS OUR DRIVEWAY!

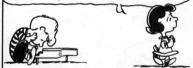

I DON'T KNOW WHY I ACCEPT WOODSTOCK'S STUPID BREAKFAST INVITATIONS

WELL, I'M HERE! WHAT ARE WE HAVING?

I KNEW IT! ONE CROUTON WITH GRAPE JELLY!

RATS!

HE WHO LIVES BY THE DIRTY ROTTEN LITTLE DROP SHOT, DIES BY THE DIRTY ROTTEN LITTLE DROP SHOT!

SORRY, MA'AM..I CAN'T RAISE MY HEAD...

MAYBE IF YOU WALKED AROUND TO THE SIDE OF THE ROOM AND STOOD THERE JUST A LITTLE TO THE LEFT OF THE RADIATOR..

HOW DID YOU DO ON THE TEST, SIR?

I GOT TWO RIGHT OUT OF TWENTY

THAT WASN'T VERY GOOD, SIR...

FROM ALL I'VE HEARD, MARCIE, IT'S LONELY AT THE TOP!

WHO, ME?

WHOM, I?

YES, MA'AM..I HAVE MY REPORT READY

THIS IS THE CLASSIC STORY OF PETER RABBIT AND HIS COAT OF MANY COLORS

HIS BROTHERS HATED HIM SO WHEN HE LOST HIS COAT OF MANY COLORS WHILE CLIMBING OVER THE FARMER'S FENCE, THEY SOLD HIM TO THE PHARAOH IN EGYPT!

THIS IS A STORY OF JEALOUSY, DESIRE AND FORGIVENESS, AND SHOULD BE A LESSON TO US ALL!

THANK YOU

PSST! WHY DID THE TEACHER HAVE SUCH A FUNNY LOOK ON HER FACE?

MAYBE SHE DOESN'T FEEL WELL

WAIT UNTIL TOMORROW WHEN I RECITE ANOTHER CLASSIC, "THE OWL AND THE FUSSY CAT"

WOMEN SHOULDN'T BE THE ONLY ONES TO CRY

MEN SHOULD REALIZE THAT IT'S ALL RIGHT FOR THEM TO CRY, TOO...

FIRST YOU HAVE TO HAVE SOMETHING HAPPEN!

I CAN UNDERSTAND WHY SOME PEOPLE LIKE TO LIVE BY THE OCEAN

THE SOUND OF THE WAVES AT NIGHT CAN BE VERY SOOTHING

THE SAME SORT OF THING SOMETIMES HELPS ME...

I'M LULLED TO SLEEP BY THE SOUND OF THE WAVES LAPPING AGAINST THE SIDE OF MY WATER DISH

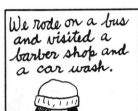

I THINK I'VE DISCOVERED SOMETHING

WHEN YOU WAKE UP AT NIGHT, AND YOUR HEAD HURTS AND YOUR STOMACH FEELS FUNNY...

THE FIRST THING YOU DO IS PUT ON YOUR BATHROBE

THEN YOU DRINK A GLASS OF WATER AND TAKE SOME PILLS, AND YOU SIT BY YOURSELF IN THE DARK FOR A WHILE UNTIL YOU'RE READY TO GO BACK TO BED...

BUT IT'S NOT THE PILLS THAT MADE YOU FEEL BETTER..

IT'S THE BATHROBE!

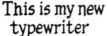
This is my new typewriter

It has many typefaces.

IT CAN ALSO cross out mistakes.

WHAT ARE YOU DOING, SIR?

QUIET, MARCIE...I'M TRYING TO MAKE THE TEACHER BELIEVE I'M THINKING...

IF SHE BELIEVES THAT, SHE'LL BELIEVE ANYTHING

SARCASM, MARCIE, WILL TURN YOUR TONGUE INTO A CARROT STICK!

..MIX TOGETHER AND ADD SLOWLY ONE CUP SELF RISING FLOUR TO MIX...

DO NOT MAKE BATTER TOO SOFT..IT MUST DROP FROM A TABLESPOON INTO HOT FAT ABOUT ONE INCH DEEP IN FRYING PAN...

HOW CAN YOU THINK ZUCCHINI FRITTERS AND STILL GET DOG FOOD?

Dear Santa Claus, How have you been?

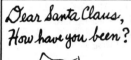

I FEEL LIKE AN IDIOT WRITING TO SOMEONE WHO DOESN'T EXIST

ON THE OTHER HAND, IF HE REALLY DOES EXIST AND I DON'T WRITE, I'D FEEL EVEN DUMBER!

THIS IS THE TIME OF YEAR WHEN IT'S BEST TO TOUCH ALL BASES

WHATEVER THAT MEANS

MA'AM?

NO, I DON'T HAVE ANY IDEA

I'M AFRAID MY BRAIN HAS LEFT FOR THE DAY

WOULD YOU CARE TO LEAVE A MESSAGE WITH THE ANSWERING SERVICE?

"AND THERE WERE IN THE SAME COUNTRY SHEPHERDS ABIDING IN THE FIELDS"

THIS OTHER TRANSLATION SAYS, "THAT NIGHT SOME SHEPHERDS WERE IN THE FIELD"

I THINK I LIKE "ABIDING" BETTER

SO DO I... ABSOLUTELY! MUCH BETTER!

WHAT DOES "ABIDING" MEAN?

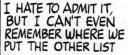

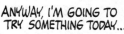

YES, MA'AM?

WHAT WAS THE NAME OF THE KING WHOSE DAUGHTER'S MARRIAGE MADE POSSIBLE THE UNIFICATION OF DENMARK AND NORWAY IN 1380?

WOW! THAT'S THE KIND OF QUESTION THAT MAKES YOUR TEMPLES THROB..

IT MAKES YOUR EARS RING AND YOUR HAIR STAND ON END...

IT MAKES YOUR EYES WATER, YOUR CHEEKS BURN, YOUR MOUTH TURN DRY AND YOUR TEETH ACHE...

A QUESTION LIKE THAT CAN DESTROY YOUR WHOLE HEAD!

CHARLIE BROWN, DO YOU THINK I WASN'T INVITED TO A NEW YEAR'S PARTY BECAUSE I'M TOO CRABBY?

NO, YOU WERE PROBABLY INVITED TO NINE PARTIES, BUT ALL THE INVITATIONS WERE LOST IN THE MAIL

THAT NEVER OCCURRED TO ME..I'LL BET THAT'S JUST WHAT HAPPENED

SOMEDAY YOU'RE GOING TO LOOK AT ME LIKE THAT, AND YOUR EYES ARE GONNA STICK!

DID I SEE YOUR FAMILY TAKING DOWN YOUR CHRISTMAS TREE YESTERDAY?

ALL THE DECORATIONS AND ORNAMENTS HAVE BEEN PACKED AWAY, AND EVERYTHING CLEANED UP

HOW ABOUT YOU?

I HAVEN'T SENT OUT MY CARDS YET!

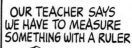

OUR TEACHER SAYS WE HAVE TO MEASURE SOMETHING WITH A RULER

HOLD STILL... I'LL TRY MEASURING YOUR MOUTH AGAIN...

HMM... ONE LIP IS ON THE SIX AND THE OTHER LIP IS ON THE NINE...

I WONDER HOW YOU WRITE THAT... I'LL PUT, "LIP TO LIP, THREE INCHES"

I CAN'T STAND IT!

RULERS HAVE OTHER USES, YOU KNOW

SEE? IF YOU TAKE YOUR PEN AND GO ALONG THE EDGE OF THE RULER, AND THEN LIFT IT UP, YOU'LL HAVE A NICE STRAIGHT...

...SMUDGE!